IT'S A
NEW
DAY!

Bob Street

EGON

EGON PUBLISHERS LTD

Acknowledgements

This book would not have been written without the initiative of Barbara Gleadhill, whose encouragement, typing skills and dedication to task have been greatly appreciated by the author. The author also wishes to record his appreciation of the friendship and encouragement given by the BBC Radio Norfolk staff.

First published in Great Britain in 1996 by
Egon Publishers Ltd, Royston Road, Baldock, Herts SG7 6NW

ISBN 1 899998 08 X

Cover design by Gill Cox

Printed in Great Britain for the publishers by Streetsprinters, Royston Road, Baldock, Herts SG7 6NW

FOREWORD

by The Rt. Rev Peter Nott, Bishop of Norwich

The Salvation Army is well known for its commitment to serving the poor in society throughout the world. But the poor consist not only of those who suffer from material poverty. There are also the 'poor in spirit' - or, as the NEB puts it - 'those who know their need of God'. The Salvation Army is deeply committed to alleviating that poverty also.

Bob Street has the gift of conveying profound truths through simple stories, and this book contains a marvellous collection of those stories, first told in the early morning to listeners to Radio Norfolk.

Bob and I, together with other Christian leaders of all the churches in East Anglia, meet regularly together as good friends and fellow workers for the Gospel of Christ. It is a joy and a privilege to commend this book, which is full of human warmth, deep truth and the humour his friends know well.

+Peter Norvic

About the Author

Bob Street became a Salvation Army officer with his wife Janet in 1969, two years after their marriage. They took charge of Salvation Army work in Droitwich for the next three years, before an appointment to the Army's editorial department in London gave Bob the opportunity to develop writing and broadcasting skills.

Subsequent service has included 10 years as editor of the Army's newspaper *The War Cry* and a period as editor-in-chief.

Corps appointments at Harpenden and Rugby gave valuable first hand experience of serving the community and meeting people at their point of need.

In 1991 Bob became Divisional Commander, Eastern Counties, and has enjoyed two years as Chairman of Norfolk Churches Together.

Bob and Janet have three children - Nicola, Mark and Tony.

Introduction

One of the most enjoyable parts of my ministry is talking to people in everyday terms about The Gospel. To have that opportunity at regular intervals on the radio is a special bonus.

In this book I have shared some of the scripts which I have used to bring aspects of the Christian life to radio listeners.

As you read the scripts you will see that I have frequently left them in the setting of the day on which they were broadcast. I hope this retains some of the freshness of the original talk and helps the reader gain something of the true aim behind what was being said in the studio.

The Gospel has something to say of worth to every area of life. These scripts touch upon some of them. I hope they will set you thinking and as a consequence you will find a measure of inspiration for your own heart and life.

Robert Street
Norwich 1996

All royalties from the sale of this book will be donated to the Salvation Army's ministry among street children in deprived areas of the world's major cities.

1
It's a new day!

LIFE is full of new experiences and five weeks ago I became a grandad. Our daughter Nicola now has a daughter of her own. Together with her husband Matthew she is just discovering what a big difference having a baby makes to your life.

It's 25 years since my wife and I found out what it was like to be responsible for a child of our own and, as Nicola is the oldest of our children, we have always made the excuse that we have had to practice on her. She hasn't always been impressed by this argument, but she is now undoubtedly 'practising' on Rebecca.

I've been surprised at how easily I've turned into a doting grandparent and, one of the things I've found fascinating, is looking into the face of this brand new infant and recognising looks and expressions that I used to see in her mother when she was a child. That being so, I am now asking myself if *our* daughter will get a taste of what it was like for us to bring her up. I have a strong suspicion (and hope!) that she will.

Nicola was always an early riser as a child and soon after she learned to walk and talk she developed the habit of running into our bedroom at some unearthly hour and announcing - with great enthusiasm - 'It's a new day!'

Her eagerness was sometimes in stark contrast to

our sleepy reluctance to get out of bed, but her chirpy little saying has become a light-hearted family motto - especially when any new day in question promises to be more demanding or troublesome than we would wish.

Well, today is another new day. For each of us it holds something different.

Like any other, it will be unpredictable, and bring tragedy and triumph, laughter and tears, hope and despair.

A few days ago I had the unspeakable pleasure of taking my new granddaughter in my arms in a Salvation Army service and dedicating her young life to God in accordance with her parents' wishes. They want her to have the chance to know God's love and friendship through each new day.

And if I have a prayer for today, it is that more and more people will realise that this love and friendship really exists - and that it is for everybody....*every* day.

Today's Text: Romans 6:4 'As Christ was raised up from the dead by the glory of the Father, even so we also should walk in newness of life.' (AV)

2
The best possible start

DURING the football season I often have my ear glued to a radio on a Saturday afternoon to hear how my football team is getting on. But, having been in editorial work for a good number of years, I can't help editing what the commentators say. I don't consciously do it, it's just that they say the most ridiculous things - regularly. I appreciate they don't have time to think about what they're saying, but they often come out with the same old cliches week after week, and I reckon they could do with a bit of advice.

For instance, almost every Saturday one of the reporters will say that some team has got off to the 'best possible start'. It may be a goal after five minutes or seven minutes, or something like that. But that doesn't make it the *best* possible start. A goal after two minutes would have been better, so a goal after five can't be the best.

Or they might suggest that a team going down by two goals after 10 minutes is the 'worst possible' start. Well it's not. They could, however unlikely, go three down after 10 minutes and have their goalie back in the dressing room with two broken legs.

There are other criticisms which the commentators 'so richly deserve', but I'd better make a positive point instead.

3

Sometimes it just isn't possible to find the right words to describe what's happening, not only on football pitches, but also when something spectacular happens, or something affects us deeply. The commentator who suddenly found the Hindenburg in flames above him knew all about that.

Poets and hymn writers through the years have grappled to find the right way of expressing all kinds of moods and feelings - and they've done it with varying degrees of success.

When it comes to describing what it's like to discover the love of God, many people have found it hard to put into words. Some might say it has to be experienced to be believed. One songwriter expressed it this way:

> But what to those who find? ah! This
> Nor tongue nor pen can show;
> The love of Jesus, what it is
> None but his loved ones know.

One other thing. To wake up knowing you are in God's love and care whatever happens, really does give you the *best* possible start, every day.

Today's text: 2 Corinthians 9:15 'Thanks be to God for his gift beyond words.' (NEB)

4

3
Gordon Wilson

A FEW years ago Gordon Wilson was neither famous nor seeking fame. He was known as a good man in his local community at Enniskillen, Northern Ireland, but even in his wildest dreams he wouldn't have expected to become a world figure, renowned for advocating peace and reconciliation.

Sadly, tragically, he found himself in the limelight when his daughter Marie was killed by an IRA bomb at Enniskillen on Remembrance Day 1987. Her dying words, as she lay in the rubble - 'Daddy, I love you very much' - were spoken as she clutched his hand.

It was no wonder the world wanted to know Gordon Wilson's reactions.

Contrary to nearly all reports Gordon Wilson did not speak initially of forgiveness - a point he makes strongly in his book *Marie*. He spoke of feeling 'no bitterness' and of having 'prayed sincerely' for his daughter's killers.

For him there was no sense in vengeance. The tragedy had occurred. Instead, he saw sense in working for peace and reconciliation, in trying to achieve understanding among people who usually weren't listening to what anybody else had to say.

He was to suffer great disappointment. After meeting IRA representatives following the Warrington bombing, he seemed to have got nowhere. He even described himself as 'naive'. Yet his determined efforts to win the hearts of people who seemed only to be fired by hatred, were an inspiration to the world. They will continue to be so.

Now he is dead. A heart attack has claimed him. And our hearts go out to his widow, Joan, who recently lost her son Peter too.

In words of tribute Irish President Mary Robinson commented that Gordon Wilson has left behind an 'important and enduring legacy'.

He has reminded us of the higher values of life - of the command of Jesus to love our enemies. And he has shown - amid great pain and heartache, which should never be taken for granted - that it is possible to put such love into practice.

Gordon Wilson would also want to remind us that such love is possible only by the strength and grace of God, to whom he always turned for help.

Today's text: *Matthew 5:43 'You have heard that it was said, 'Love your neighbour and hate your enemy.' But I tell you, 'Love your enemies and pray for those who persecute you, that you may be the sons of your Father in Heaven.' '* (NIV)

4
Nelson's Example

WHEN it was 'all over' I realised that on every occasion I had been in the wrong place at the wrong time. No matter how I tried to work it, the fact was I'd needed to be in certain places at certain times - and I missed nearly all the lot.

What am I talking about? The Rugby World Cup 1995, won by South Africa on their own soil.

But there were some things - away from the Rugby itself - which have left a lasting impression. As an Englishman it hurts me to say it, but I thought Gavin Hastings was a very special kind of ambassador for Scotland. He'd have made me proud to be Scottish. But, as I'm English, I'll content myself with the memory of the 'last kick' victory over Australia.

The real highlight came on Saturday, when the final was over and South Africa had won. There was Nelson Mandela wearing a South African rugby jersey, identifying himself totally with what used to be a game exclusively for whites. He was actually wearing the jersey which used to symbolise division.

This time South Africa's president was using it to symbolise unity - a unity in which he has played no small part.

It was less than five years ago that Nelson Mandela was still in prison serving year after year for having the courage to stand for the rights which he believed belonged to his people.

Following his release he boldly and tactfully negotiated the dawn of a new era to replace the dark days of apartheid. Then he became President. So what did he do? Gain revenge? Get his own back? Not a bit of it. He spoke of reconciliation. Of forgiveness. Of unity. Of working together. Of one nation.

He had to carry the judgment of people from all sides who were bent on other, less honourable solutions.

Well, last Saturday - admittedly a day for South Africa to rejoice - the world saw a nation that had grown together. The people had been given an example and they'd followed it.

I suggest that next time we feel *we've* been wronged, when we want to get our own back, when we don't want to forgive - it'll be worth turning our thoughts to Nelson Mandela, whose inspirational leadership is worth much more than ten thousand world cups.

Today's text: Matthew 6:14 'If you forgive men when they sin against you, your heavenly Father will also forgive you. But if you do not forgive men their sins, your Father will not forgive your sins.' (NIV)

5
'Hard men' pray

THOSE of you who were listening in yesterday will know that when I'd finished my comments on the Rugby World Cup, Jim, our friendly Radio Norfolk morning presenter, mentioned that fact that the entire South African rugby team had knelt down and prayed as soon as the final whistle had gone, and they knew they'd won the cup.

That comment set me thinking again - for several reasons. First of all, there's the fact that we rarely see a group of people kneel in prayer spontaneously. But second, what I find significant is that they were men. Men are much more reserved (as a rule) about owning up to a faith and being prepared to witness to it in public.

Yet we can go a step further here, because these were your actual 'hard men', rugby men, macho men. And they knelt and prayed, unashamedly and without embarrassment.

What they did cut across the superficial media image of Christians being wimps, or soft and wet - and that Christianity is only for weak people who can't cope with life.

Another significant aspect of their action was that they were saying 'thanks' to God. They weren't asking him to do them favours. They weren't praying for him to let them win.

And that helped put right another misconception

- that saying our prayers is mainly about asking God to make everything turn out right for us.

Prayer is about finding the strength from God to live a good life - to have the courage to do what's right when it's easier to do what's wrong. It's about learning from God what we should be doing rather than telling God what we want him to do for us. And the more we think about it the more we can see that tough grown men saying their prayers actually makes sense.

And as for saying 'thank you'...well, they reminded us that we ought not to take the good things for granted, or take too much pride in our own achievements. Because when we do well, we only do so by using the talents God has given us in the first place.

Today's text: *Luke 11:1* *'One day Jesus was praying in a certain place. When he finished, one of his disciples said to him, 'Lord, teach us how to pray.' '* *(NIV)*

6
A world of difference

A GOVERNMENT minister recently 'put the cat among the pigeons' by stating that parents who just live together are four times as likely to split up than those who are married. He said that whatever people's views about 'living in sin' - and he didn't want to comment along those lines - children are usually given the most stable upbringing if their parents are married. He produced the figures to back up what he was saying.

Yesterday child specialist Professor Charles Brooke revealed the results of his research into how children respond to love, care and security - and among his more startling findings was the statement that giving children hugs actually helps them grow. Youngsters who do not feel loved produce less growth hormone, he said.

Today there has been another survey report - and that's about begging. While it said that some beggars are making £200 a week, a national charity drew attention to the fact that 80 per cent or so are begging because they can't survive on the benefits they receive from the state. And here's the telling statistic - 50 per cent of beggars are young people who used to be in care. When they 'became of age' they had no security, nowhere to go, nowhere where they belonged. No hugs.

So the word leaping out for our consideration is the word 'care'. We all respond better for being cared for and if we are let down regularly in this respect, all kinds of problems set in. Our care is basic to our wellbeing and childhood days are especially significant.

It isn't surprising that the United Nations declared 1994 as the International Year of the Family, because whatever our political persuasion we can't escape the fact that society needs families - families that care.

They will always come in different shapes and sizes. They will always have problems. They will always be less than perfect. But if the caring is there they will eventually make a world of difference.

Today's text: Matthew 25:35-40 'I was hungry and you gave me something to eat, I was thirsty and you gave me something to drink. I was a stranger and you invited me in, I needed clothes and you clothed me, I was sick and you looked after me, I was in prison and you came to visit me.'

'Then the righteous will answer him...'When?...The king will reply... 'Whatever you did for one of the least of these brothers of mine, you did for me.' ' (NIV)

7
No

MY wife and I have three children. Perhaps two is too nice and four is too many. I don't know, but in our experience by the time we'd got to our third child we were being worn down at the edges a bit. I mean, you don't feel like being so strict.

You've spent a fair bit of time telling your first two children why they shouldn't do this and why they can't do that and you don't feel like going through it all again.

Saying 'No' can become tiresome, so there's a temptation to say 'Yes' more often for the youngest of your offspring.

If my memory serves me right it was 'Bomber' Harris who, in the war, told his officers that when forces personnel were seeking permission for compassionate leave or some special exemption they - the officers - could only say 'Yes'. If they thought the answer should be 'No' they had to refer it back to him. He would then say 'No' if that was what he felt the answer should be. What he didn't want was any over-bossy officers saying 'No' unnecessarily.

When God gives a 'No' answer we sometimes find it hard to accept. We take it personally - as if he's never said 'No' before - and some of us decide he doesn't care, or even exist.

So it's worth remembering that God said 'No' three times to the Apostle Paul and also to his own son, Jesus. Three times Jesus asked his Father God if it was possible for him to be released from the horror of being crucified. Three times the answer from a loving father was 'No'. Although Jesus felt forsaken it didn't leave him bitter. He accepted that the answer was for our good. When he prayed his prayer to be excused he concluded with - 'Nevertheless, not what I want, but what you will.'

Next time you get a 'No' from God, it might be worth talking to Jesus about it.

Today's text: 2 Corinthians 12:9   'There was given me a thorn in my flesh to torment me. Three times I pleaded with the Lord to take it away from me. But he said to me, 'My grace is sufficient for you.' ' (NIV)

8
Something in common

THE other day a young friend asked me if I knew what Attila the Hun and Winnie the Pooh had in common. Well, I didn't. If there was any connection between a fifth century barbarian and a fictional, inoffensive bear, I certainly couldn't see it. Then came the answer. Attila *the* Hun and Winnie *the* Pooh have the same middle name!

Now, it might take some of us longer than others to work out that the middle name they share is 'the' - but whoever thought up the joke actually did me a favour. He set me thinking about the possibilities of more unlikely people who might find something in common if they tried hard enough.

Not so long ago the Palestinians and Israelis found *they* had something in common after years of mistrust, killings and conflict. What they had was a desire for peace. It was such an unlikely event that people's hopes for other troubled areas began to rise.

Progress made in Northern Ireland in 1994 came about because, with all kinds of unspeakable acts of violence going on, some people still believed most citizens wanted peace.

Prophets of doom in South Africa also discovered that God was at work in men's hearts, and common ground was not only found, but shared.

What about ourselves? Aren't there times when

we need to look for the good in people we don't naturally like, in the hope that we'll find *some* shared hope or interest?

Recently a BBC reporter said of a nation which didn't seem remotely interested in moving towards peace and reconciliation: 'They never miss an opportunity to miss an opportunity.'

Let's make sure we take *our* opportunities for promoting peace.

Today's text: Romans 12:18 'If possible, so far as it lies with you, live at peace with all men.' (NEB)

9
Casualty

IN the past few months, I've had cause to be grateful for hospital casualty departments. In fact, it's been as if our family has had a season ticket.

It all began with me arriving at the Norfolk and Norwich Hospital for some emergency x-rays.

But within a couple of weeks it was my wife's turn. A particularly nasty splinter down the nail of her wedding ring finger meant that it needed the touch of the experts.

Then just as we started our holiday with the family, I tore a calf muscle playing football. My lads had encouraged me to have a game of five-a-side at a holiday camp, and just when the old magic was coming back, my left leg objected to the force with which I kicked the ball at goal.

The very next day I was at the hospital again. I hobbled in on my crutches - not for myself - I was taking Matthew our son-in-law. He'd damaged his knee ligaments - also playing football.

Within a week I was back visiting another casualty department. This time our sons Tony and Mark had jumped to head the football and they'd clashed heads. Mark tore his lip. Tony tore his chin. Tony needed stitching up. (Dangerous game this football.)

We could have been forgiven for thinking we'd had our fair share of accidents, but just a couple of months later Tony managed to hit a car with his motor bike while going at a fair speed on a main road. He went over the car and landed on the other side of the highway. Casualty sorted him out - and we were very grateful that he came out of it alive - and with no bones broken.

Soon after this I arranged a survey of 'teens and twenties' to see how many of them had broken a bone at some time or another. Thirty-six per cent had managed it, while 54 per cent - more than half - had needed stitches at some time. I also found out that 20 per cent were responsible for breaking somebody else's bones.

In a wider sense we are all casualties, and it's pretty certain we are all to blame for causing hurt to others as well - not necessarily by breaking bones, but by being less than we ought to be, by hitting out in anger or perhaps by being thoughtless.

Jesus was called the Great Healer, and he's on record as inviting all of us carrying deep hurts to bring them to him. If you're carrying hurts today - hurts that make you feel like a casualty - get to know the Great Healer and take him at his word.

Today's text: *Matthew 11:28,29* *'Come to me, all of you who are weary and overburdened, and I will give you rest. Put on my yoke and learn from me. For I am gentle and humble in heart and you will find rest for your souls.'* (J.B. Phillips)

10
Me against me

FROM the age of seven Ian Botham was convinced he was going to be a famous sportsman. What he didn't know was, what kind? At 15 he had offers from Crystal Palace and five other football league clubs, but he ended up going to Lords as a trainee cricketer.

He says that all through his life he has possessed an extraordinary self-belief. His cricketing achievements bear witness to that. But he also confesses in his autobiography that he has never liked to admit a mistake. This greatest of cricketers is apparently well-known among his team mates as being legendary for devising incredible excuses for being out. He just hasn't wanted to face the truth.

In the business of not wanting to admit our failures, Ian Botham isn't alone. Most of us seem to possess a great reluctance to admit to our shortcomings - but they need to be faced. In this respect Ian could be setting us a good example.

Apparently he likes to go for long walks on his own to take time to think, and chew things over. That's one of the reasons why he enjoys his long treks to raise money to fight leukaemia. He describes the thinking that goes on in his mind while on these walks as 'Me against me'.

Botham will always be known as a great fighter, a warhorse, the most formidable of opponents. But in the battles we all fight in life the greatest one is always with ourselves. Me against me.

No matter how much we disagree with others, or point the finger or take on the rest, the fact remains that, first and foremost, we need to control ourselves - to win the battle against our worst self. We need to fight to become the person God - our Creator - intended us to be and knows we can be.

This battle is for all of us. It brings a new challenge to every day. Me against me! May the best person win.

Today's text: 2 Corinthians 13:5 'Examine yourselves: are you living the life of faith? Put yourselves to the test.' (NEB)

11
Blinded with science

I'VE never quite been able to work out why some people think science and Christianity don't mix. It's as if they think one disproves the other - and that's nonsense.

We've known for some time of the existence of black holes and that the galaxies of which we are aware probably form only one-tenth of the entire universe. But now we are being introduced to a new class of 'black objects'.

Hydrogen and helium feature prominently in their make up, but the *number* of these objects seems to be the most impressive piece of information. Apparently there are 10 million billion of them.

There's obviously a good deal more to learn about these failed stars, and there's a vast amount of speculation as to their value within the universe. But at least it gives the scientists something at which to point their telescopes.

Not so long ago, two famous scientists, Professor Fred Hoyle and Professor Chandra Wickramasinghe, set out to *disprove* the existence of God.

As they examined the laws which govern our existence they amazed themselves by coming to the conclusion that evidence for a creator was overwhelming.

Their research led them to issue a report which said that the chances of the world being an accident were a mere 10 to the power of 40,000. For those of us who don't know what this means - even with a calculator - they said it meant that the chances of the world being an accident were 'so utterly minuscule as to make it absurd.'

Professor Hoyle said proof of a creator at work was to be found in 'masses of evidence of *designer* activity that is continuing to sustain the universe.'

Belief in a creator is one thing. The next step is to ask ourselves *why* he put us here and what do we mean to him? To go through life without trying to get answers is to miss the best exploration (and discovery) of all.

Today's text Psalm 8:3 *'When I consider your heavens, the work of your fingers, the moon and the stars which you have set in place, what is man, that you are mindful of him?'* (NIV)

12
Don't run away

ONE of the saddest stories in Britain recently was of a 14-year-old girl who ran away from her community home, went for a 'joy ride' and was killed in the subsequent crash.

On the same day there was a televised debate about running away and children playing truant from school. Nobody had all the answers because there's more than one reason why children do these things.

But children aren't the only ones who play truant. Today a few thousand adults will feign illness and stay away from work. Most won't get caught and they'll justify their actions by calling it one of their sick days.

Some people play truant from church. They decide it's too much effort to get out of bed on a Sunday, or they reckon it's just not relevant enough.

Perhaps more sensitively we need to acknowledge that some parents might be playing truant on their children. They are not there when they are needed, and not always for unavoidable reasons.

Running away has always been with us, but it isn't often a good idea, because whether we run away from home, work, school or church we still have to face ourselves.

I doubt if many people would openly admit it, but there's a large percentage running away from God. We never quite get round to telling him he's not welcome. We just keep him at a distance and fill our time with one thing and another, never really daring to stop and find out what he has to tell us.

The psalmist knew this, and he wrote that there was absolutely nowhere he could run to, that would get him out of God's sight. So, he decided, 'What's the point of running? Let's face up to him!'

And when he did that, he discovered that what or who he had been frightened of, actually turned out to be his greatest security.

Today's text: *Psalm 139:7-23 'Where can I go from your Spirit? Where can I flee from your presence? ...Search me, O God, and know my heart. (NIV)*

13
Just my luck!

ON my wedding day, just as I was adding those
final touches to my curly locks, I managed to knock
the mirror. It fell from the wall and broke into
several pieces on the floor. Whether you're
superstitious or not you probably know that it's said
that this means seven years bad luck.

One day I met an old lady who believed this so
much that she insisted I should never have got
married. It was an omen she said. Very definitely
seven years bad luck. Well, I've been married for
four times that long now and I'm glad to report the
bad luck never came.

While our daughter was having her photographs
taken on *her* wedding day, a bird, sitting in a tree
above her, decided to deposit what it didn't want
right on her wedding dress. Now that's supposed to
be *good* luck. But it wasn't for me, because I had
to clear the mess up and make her dress look
brilliant white again. Even so, when you're getting
married it's no good depending on luck.

Although a lot of the old superstitions have died
away it's also noticeable that in parts of England
their influence lives on. It isn't only black cats,
horse shoes, not walking under ladders, keeping new
shoes off the table, turning your money over in your
pocket when you hear a cuckoo, saying 'Touch
wood', or believing that things happen in threes.

25

We also have the stars to claim our attention as well. Although the daily papers frequently contradict each other with their predictions some people still believe other forces are controlling our destiny.

When we reject or avoid the Christian faith, we usually find a substitute to fill up the religious gap in our life. But substitutes are never quite the same. Superstitions and stars don't help meet our deepest needs. They can't. Only God can.

The apostle Paul was certain of this. He wrote. 'I am convinced that neither death nor life, neither angels nor demons, neither the present nor the future, nor any powers, neither height nor depth (*stars in their ascendancy or descendency*) nor anything else in all creation will be able to separate us from the love of God that is in Christ Jesus our Lord.' Faith like that is a lot better than luck!

Today's text: Psalm 13:5 'I trust in your unfailing love; my heart rejoices in your salvation.' (NIV)

14
National Hug Week

IT was National Hug Week in Britain and two main charities linked up to encourage everyone to give a hug to people who wouldn't normally get one. Apparently 37 per cent of people questioned reckoned that they miss out on hugs - and hugs are important to us all. They make us feel loved - that we belong.

I'm sure that's true, and I supported the campaign, but I found it all somewhat ironic. You see, my 17-year-old son, who likes to test his strength against his father - decided to see if he was stronger than me. So he gave me a bear hug.

It was all supposed to be friendly. He squeezed and squeezed, and waited to see if I would plead for mercy or something. Actually, I didn't plead for mercy, but I did crack - literally. One of my ribs gave way and he realised he'd applied just too much pressure. What was intended as a friendly hug ended with someone getting hurt. Me!

So perhaps it was a good idea that during National Hug Week, we were given the opportunity to *send* people a hug, rather than necessarily break their ribs proving we cared. Cards were on sale - they would be, wouldn't they! - so you could send your hug to someone you cared about but couldn't be with. Money raised from the cards went to the charities mentioned, so even more people could feel loved.

The pain I felt for a few weeks reminded me that some people apply *too much* pressure (emotional or otherwise) to the people for whom they are supposedly caring. They overpower them, possessively, because they are basically meeting their *own* needs, and that isn't healthy.

While some of us enjoy playing happy families - and thank God happy families do exist - it's all too easy to neglect acquaintances who could do with knowing and feeling they are valued too.

When Jesus emphasised the commandment that we should love our neighbour as ourselves, he was effectively telling us to include everyone - the unlovely as well. We are to give a hug to the whole world.

Significantly, God doesn't overpower us with a bear-like hug. Our arms aren't trapped by our sides as he takes us into his care. He gives us the freedom to choose to receive his love, and the opportunity to put our arms round him in response.

Today's text: 1 John 4:12 'If we love one another, God lives in us and his love is made complete in us.' (NIV)

15
Hidden goods - hidden feelings

ACCORDING to recent news reports there was a 79-year-old widow who was said to have gone on a massive shopping spree that lasted for 17 years.

When she was finally caught it was discovered that the value of the goods she had stolen was £60,000. Nearly all the 7,000 items were neatly stacked in their original wrappers.

Among the goods she was said to have taken were 418 hats, 203 belts, 236 pairs of gloves, 843 jumpers, 169 handbags, 448 pairs of shoes, 394 coats, 711 skirts, 1370 scarves and 749 blouses.

There's more - such as 332 necklaces, 421 pairs of earrings, 25 umbrellas, a six-foot high clothes drier, a fire extinguisher and a *wheelbarrow*. I presume you'd need something to carry it all home in.

Apparently it took 12 hours, seven policemen and six large vans to remove the goods...which were then given to The Salvation Army for distribution in the Developing World.

The police decided not to press charges. A spokesman said, 'She was lonely, upset and *unable to help herself*.' I was glad that they saw beyond the obvious. People who enjoy pointing the finger, condemning out of hand and throwing the book at others, don't usually help matters and have often got something to hide themselves. People who - like the police on this occasion - are generous and gentle with their correction, seem to have remembered that all of us need special understanding at one time or another.

According to reports, the woman's irrational behaviour began when her husband died.

Although we smile incredulously at the thought of an elderly lady managing to fool everybody for so long, we also recognise that her deep need for love and understanding wasn't properly identified for 17 years.

It would seem she had hidden her feelings as well as she had hidden the goods. We don't know. Perhaps we should ask God for a perception that cares enough to look beyond the obvious and identify the needs we could meet just where we are.

Today's text: Psalm 103:13   'As a father has compassion on his children...so the Lord has compassion on those who fear him.' (NIV)

16
What's in it for me?

THE televising of Parliamentary debates in London might seem as exciting as watching paint dry, but occasionally we get some high drama.

I arrived home one night just in time to see the 10pm voting on the Maastricht Treaty in the House of Commons. It was passionate stuff, because the Government's plans to take the UK into Europe were in jeopardy.

On the way home my car radio told me that the Government might avoid defeat because the Prime Minister John Major had struck a last minute deal with the Ulster Unionists. Their votes, it was suggested, would be bought for certain concessions. Some people said it was an arrangement which had a 'what's in it for me' flavour. Nobody seemed to know whether or not it was true.

Earlier this week a national newspaper said that loyalty in football was dead, and it implied that players and managers had a 'what's in it for me' attitude. It went on to deride 'loyalty bonuses' - especially for players who were currently said to be wanting £150,000 before they would leave one club for another.

But now we hear that it may soon become law for people selling insurance to tell the rest of us how much commission they will get when we sign up for them. They're actually going to have to *tell us* what's in it for them! That should be different.

I'm sure it's just as well we can't strike deals with God - though some of us try. 'I'll do that for you if you do this for me,' we say. But we can't buy his favour. We can't earn it or work for it.

The fact is, God's love for us is free. Yet it can only be enjoyed if we put aside our demands and deals, and accept him wholeheartedly into our lives - no strings.

What's in it for us if we turn to God with nothing but an open heart? Jesus called it 'life in all its fullness'. That's what!

Today's text: *Matthew 10:39 'By gaining his life, a man will lose it; by losing his life for my sake, he will gain it.'* (NIV)

17
Your money or your life

DURING the past couple of weeks I've knocked on a lot more doors than usual. The Salvation Army has been making its Annual Appeal and I've been playing my part with the collection.

You learn a lot about people when you knock on their doors and ask them all the same question. My overriding impression is that Norfolk folk are kindly and thoughtful, and ready to help, even though money may not be plentiful.

Hardly anyone gave me a point blank refusal to help - just one chap who had a detached house with a double garage. I'd have liked to have asked him why he refused - perhaps to satisfy my curiosity - but especially because his negative response stood out like a sore thumb. I also met quite a few elderly people - and some not so elderly - who seemed to be frightened to open their door to anyone. This kind of fear was absent 20 years ago. Now it's everywhere.

Overwhelmingly, people made me feel they were glad to see me - glad to see the Sally Army uniform - and glad to support the work. It reminded me that The Salvation Army has a lot to live up to if it's to 'keep up the good work' in the way the public wants.

This year scores of people from outside The Salvation Army have joined in and helped us. It's been a good move. We've got to know more people that way. And they've got to know more about what makes us tick.

From my own point of view, I've often wanted to take longer to chat to people on their doorsteps, especially when I've sensed some are awake to the wider work in which they could get involved.

It was Dick Turpin, the notorious highwayman, who is said to have used the phrase, 'Your money or your life', but I'd like to steal it for The Salvation Army this morning. After all, why should the devil have all the best lines?

The fact is, when it comes to helping in this world, God needs us to give more than our money. 'Your money *and* your life' might be a more appropriate slogan. Because it's only in giving God our lives that we discover just how much richer and fulfilling he can make them.

Today's text: Matthew 6:20 'Store up for yourselves treasures in heaven, where moth and rust do not destroy, and where thieves do not break in and steal. For where your treasure is, there will your heart be also.' (NIV)

18
Short memories

I'M not an expert on goldfish but I've fed one or two in my time, and I've certainly cleaned out a few tanks and bowls on behalf of our children. But I recently came across a priceless piece of information about them. According to those who know, goldfish have memories that only last for two seconds.

Just think about it! While I've been concerned that the poor little fish only had a small tank or bowl to swim in, the fish had *no idea* that he'd swum there before. In fact, all the time he's swimming round and round he keeps thinking everywhere's new. Life must be wonderfully exciting for him!

It isn't so exciting if you're a person who knows your memory is going. And it was brave of President Regan to speak out not so long ago to tell us that he was now suffering from Alzhiemer's disease.

Our memory is a precious commodity. In many ways it makes us what we are. It keeps life's experiences in our minds. We learn from what our memory retains.

On Remembrance Sunday we were invited to put our memories into action - those of us who were old enough - and recall the sacrifice of people who died in the great wars.

The two-minute silence gave us opportunity to think other thoughts too - about recent wars, people who are maimed as a result of conflict, others who have been damaged in mind, and some whose faith in God and man has been shattered as a result of war. We had opportunity to remind ourselves of the evils of war and to quietly confirm our personal intention to live at peace with others.

The way we handle our memories is all-important as to how we make the best or worst of life. We all have good and bad memories. We've all been let down by others. We've all been helped by others. If we hold on to bad memories, keep bitterness alive, we damage ourselves more than anybody else. In fact, we cause more injury.

If we reflect on how grateful we can be for so much that has come our way - pushing aside our grudges - we'll feel a whole lot better.

The Bible tells us that if we bring our wrongdoings to God - for forgiveness - he'll forget all about them - just as if we'd done nothing wrong. He asks us to do the same for others. I don't think any of us could ask for more - and that's worth remembering for more than a couple of seconds.

Today's text: *Psalm 103:12 'As far as the east is from the west, so far has he removed our transgressions from us.'*
(NIV)

19
Cheats never prosper

I'M fascinated by how much cheating is dominating the news. Top of the list and making most of the headlines are the accusations that top footballers have accepted bribes to lose or 'fix' matches. The players concerned have strenuously denied the accusations and their friends are standing by them.

But now we are hearing that the cricketers of two championship counties have been accused of a 'trade-off' to fix the outcome of two matches at the conclusion of the 1991 season - one match each, according to what suited their interests. These accusations have again been strenuously denied.

Then last Sunday there were those who suggested that when motor racing's Michael Schumacher realised his car was damaged and Damon Hill would probably win the world motor racing championship as a consequence, he deliberately cut across Hill and effectively put him out of the race.

Wisely, Damon Hill decided not to entertain such accusations. Calling someone a cheat is a nasty business.

We don't like cheats. There's something decidedly distasteful about trying to deceive people in order to feather your own nest.

One of the most obvious and most observed ways of trying to cheat in sport is when footballers automatically raise their arms to claim a throw-in for *their* side when the ball goes out of play. It typifies an attitude of 'let's see what we can get away with' - similar to two drivers who recently hit my parked car - at different times - and left no record of who they were! They just left damage instead.

It's a way of life. But it's a way of life that leads to loss of self respect - and an excusing of ourselves from standards we expect of others.

Cheating on others breeds a lack of trust, and creates suspicion. In the end, it destroys relationships. It really isn't the way to prosper.

Today's text: Acts 5:1-4   'A man named Ananias sold a piece of property...he kept back part of the money for himself, but brought the rest to the apostles' feet.

Peter said, 'Ananias, how is it that you have lied to the Holy Spirit and have kept for yourself some of the money you received for the land?...You have not lied to me but to God." (NIV)

20
You bet!

TODAY sees the start of the national lottery. Tickets are available and it's generally reckoned that we're going to put a lot of money into the government's coffers because of it. The organisers of the lottery stand to do well too.

There are those who say that if punters are really concerned about giving to charity, they should do just that - give to charity, because only a small percentage of stake money will find its way to charitable causes. But as far as I can see, most people will enter the lottery basically to win money.

It's argued that many of those who buy tickets will be among the least able to afford it - and it's not surprising that some suggest that the top pay out of several million pounds simply can't be morally justified. Nor can encouraging a nation to waste its money for that matter.

Somebody once said that gambling was the opiate of the bored - and there's no doubt that the lottery has been promoted as something that will brighten up our lives.

A few thousand miles away in Sri Lanka, some people are doing their level best to leave nothing to chance. The recently-elected government decided the planets weren't in the right order on the day it was due to be sworn-in, so it postponed the ceremony until the next day when all the 'signs were right'. That was interesting because similar astrological considerations were given to the date of the election by the *outgoing* government - yes, the one that lost!

It was football manager Alan Ball who is reported to have said, 'I don't believe in luck, but everybody needs some.'

Well, none of us knows what's just around the corner, but my life's experience has taught me that a hand placed in the hand of God is more reliable than the best bet. It's a guarantee that whether things work out to our liking *or* go badly wrong, we have always got the help of the one who is never surprised by events, and who alone can ultimately guarantee life's most worthwhile and lasting rewards.

Today's text: *Matthew 6:33 'Seek first his kingdom and his righteousness, and all these things will be given to you as well.'* (NIV)

21
One giant leap

LIKE many others I remember where I was the moment man stepped on the moon for the first time. I was sitting in front of the television! Then we heard the immortal words, 'That's one small step for man - one giant leap for mankind.' They were spoken by Neil Armstrong. The Americans had got to the moon first.

We were all pretty excited at the time. So we should have been. But day trips to the moon haven't got any nearer - in fact, they seem to be less likely. Space exploration has boldly gone in different directions.

In 1969 it was important to have won the race to the moon, but these days Russia and America are pooling their resources and exploring space *together*. They began by planning to build a joint space station.

Joint co-operation is usually a good thing. It works well in marriages, at work, and on specific projects and adventures. The old maxim 'Two heads are better than one' generally holds good.

Churches in England co-operate with each other more than ever now - and that's got to be a good sign. There's a wider acceptance of each other's role in society and a better respect for differing views. In any case, if churches didn't co-operate with each other they'd be setting a pretty poor example.

As for co-operating with God - well, that's a personal matter. And most people would admit there are times when they'd rather not.

We've all got this tendency to do the wrong things and choose what God forbids. That's why lots of us keep him at a distance. If we get too close he might just trouble our conscience.

The Bible says we can be 'co-workers' with him. We can ask him to co-operate with us, to help make us better people.

If we each gave it a try, well, that really would be a giant leap for mankind.

Today's text: *2 Corinthians 6:1* *'As workers together with him, we urge you not to receive the grace of God in vain.'* (NIV)

22
God is wearing your shoes

AS I understand it, soon after he was deposed, former Soviet Union President Mikhail Gorbachev revealed that he couldn't manage on his pension. Apparently £100 a month wasn't enough. He and his wife Raisa found it hard to make ends meet - and this after he had been the leader of one of the world's two super powers.

It seemed ironic - especially as Mr Gorbachev, a communist, was supposedly dedicated to achieving fair shares for all. It was only when he had no power that he realised from first-hand experience what kind of problems his people had been facing for a long time. When he finally knew, he had no authority to do anything about it. All he could do was try to make ends meet.

The person who said that we should never criticise anyone else until we've walked in their shoes for a mile or two had a pretty good point. It seems that Mr Gorbachev found himself in other people's shoes too late.

The idea that God sits up in the clouds in isolated splendour went out some time ago, but it seems to me that a lot of people haven't woken up to the fact that God is very much at work, down here at the heart of things. He is ready to help, understanding the situation - from experience.

The difference between God and Gorbachev - or

at least one of them - is that the divine Lord Jesus Christ *chose* to leave the riches and splendour of glory to come to earth to live. And, in so doing, he experienced at first-hand what it was like to live life on the ground. His home wasn't special and for 30 years his way of life was nothing out of the ordinary. When he travelled around he knew what it was to be hungry, thirsty, homeless, misunderstood, unjustly condemned, to suffer - then to die a lonely death.

It would be a pity, with Jesus having all this experience and the capacity to help, if we foolishly thought that he didn't know or even care. The truth is, that whatever size shoes we are wearing, he knows what it's like to be in them.

Today's text: Hebrews 4:15 'We do not have a high priest who is unable to sympathize with our weaknesses, but we have one who has been tempted in every way, just as we are.' (NIV)

23
Holocaust victory

SEVENTY-SIX years ago the armistice which ended the First World War was signed. Something like six million people were killed during the conflict, and the trench warfare - as gruesome as it was pointless - will for ever be among the world's most shameful happenings.

Yet worse was to follow. Not many years afterwards the persecution of the Jews began to escalate. By 1945 six million Jews had been murdered by the Nazis in concentration camps around Europe.

The victory of the Second World War was tempered by the world's collective shame that it had somehow allowed all this to happen.

Last year I again visited the Holocaust memorial in Jerusalem. I had been there before and I knew the history well, but another reminder of how evil humans can be, didn't do me any harm.

One of my friends - usually a tough, no-nonsense type - left early in tears. Another friend said he couldn't help feeling guilty - he just had to accept some of the collective shame of the human race for what had happened.

He said he had to face the fact that the people who were engaged in the systematic, degrading slaughter of millions were previously regarded as normal family men - husbands, sons and loving fathers. If ever it was evident that mankind needed a Saviour he said it was in seeing this.

Our guide - a refugee Jew from Romania - had been in a concentration camp with his family when he was a teenager. He told us of the time his father was dying of starvation, and how when he was given a job in the kitchens, he took the opportunity to sneak out some food for his father.

When his father discovered where the food had come from he refused to eat it. It was contaminated - not by bacteria - but by virtue of the fact that it had been taken without consent.

Our guide marvelled at his father's principles and his faith. (He doesn't tell this story to the tour parties he guides around Israel. It is too precious.)

Among guests to his country are German tourists. Someone asked him how he felt about talking to them about the history of his nation.

'It isn't a problem for me,' he said. 'It is quite the reverse. The fact that we walk through the Holocaust memorial together and share a common despair is the real victory over all that took place.'

The world needs more victories like that - and it's only when we have each learned how to forgive, that such victories can have any lasting effect.

Today's text: *1 Corinthians 15:57 'Thanks be to God, who gives us the victory through our Lord Jesus Christ.'* (RSV)

46

24
All sunshine makes a Sahara

YEARS ago we used to think sunny days were a good thing. They were a welcome relief from our unpredictable weather, and sunbathing was a simple luxury. Things are different now.

Everywhere we turn someone is waiting to warn us to protect our skin from the sun's deadly rays. Quality sunglasses are needed to protect our eyes and hats must be worn. We're reminded not to leave our pets (or children!) in locked cars - although we're also being advised not to use our cars, because the exhaust fumes, plus the sun's heat, makes for poor air quality.

Asthma and hay fever sufferers have a much worse time these days because of poor air quality, and we're told that the best place for fresh air in the UK is the bracing east coast. All this suggests to me - living near the coast - that I should take a day off and go for a dip in the sea! Ah, if only it were that easy!

I suppose most of us know what it is to plan for a great holiday only to have it spoiled by the weather. I've never forgotten the time when we went down to Devon and hired a caravan on a farm to get away from it all - but it rained every day.

The field in which our caravan was parked became a bog, the water supply turned brown, we had *three* flat tyres on our car, I swallowed a fly, was stung by a wasp, lost every game of snakes and ladders - well, what else was there to do with a young family? - and to finish it all, my wife had raging toothache.

Then it happened! For a few brief hours the sun came out. We quickly made our way into Devon's delightful lanes and we saw the flowing rainwater glistening brightly in the new-found sunlight. The sight and sound was beautiful - and then came the rainbow. The mixture of sun and rain had produced another marvel of creation.

Someone once said (very wisely) that all sunshine makes a Sahara. Absolutely true. We need sun and rain to keep life going - even if both often occur at inconvenient times - just as we need joy and sorrow, triumph and disaster, success and failure, delight and disappointment, for a balanced life.

If we offer both the welcome and the unwelcome things to God, he'll help us find purpose in them both. And eventually, he might just make something beautiful out of us.

Today's text: *Romans 8:28 'We know that in all things God works for the good of those who love him.'* (NIV)

25
Hello, Brick Wall

IF ever anyone in our family is trying to talk to somebody else in our family, only to find the other person isn't listening, the words which eventually get through are 'Hello, brick wall.' And - however quietly spoken they may be - they usually do the trick.

I think it was my younger brother Paul who introduced the phrase to us, possibly because talking to some of us can be like talking to a brick wall.

Well, anyone who has visited Jerusalem knows it to be a place full of walls - ancient, very ancient and some modern.

In one particular place, near the Mount of Olives, there are a number of walls in a courtyard which present the Lord's Prayer in 66 different languages. We had a cursory glance at most of them, then had an intriguing discussion about the version printed in the original language. Did it say 'on earth' or 'in earth' somebody wanted to know. And did it say 'Our Father *which* art in Heaven' or '*who* art in Heaven'?

My contribution to the debate was to say that language is always changing. The meaning of words alters through the generations - and to get the *exact* translation is just about impossible.

When I arrived back from Jerusalem, on my last visit, I was intrigued to hear that the Bishop of

Norwich (Bishop Peter) had again brought the Lord's Prayer to everyone's attention. Because of the different versions available, causing possible confusion to people who might want to unite to pray, he suggested it could be best to stay with the old familiar words.

I've no quarrel with that. I'd just add that prayer doesn't have to be any particular set of words. We can talk to God anywhere, any place, any time.

While I was in Jerusalem I moved among many people who actually chose to stand in front of a wall to pray. This was the Wailing Wall and some of my friends found it a helpful place, too. It was a place where they felt able to tell God the things they wanted to share with him. I found that intriguing because, when some people can't seem to get through to God, they say it seems as if there's a wall in the way. It's like talking to a brick wall.

But prayer is a two-way thing. God wants to talk to us. I wonder, when he's trying to get through to you or me - do you think he might sometimes feel like he's talking to a brick wall too?

Today's text: *Psalm 95:7.8 'Today, if you hear his voice, do not harden your hearts.'* (NIV)

26
Misleading messages

I TRAVEL well in excess of 30,000 miles a year with my work and recently, while being driven by someone else for a change, I noticed a sign which informed us that there would be roadworks in 600 metres. Then another sign said it would be 400.

When the 400 metres were up there weren't any roadworks, but there was another sign. This one told us to slow down to 10 mph because of loose chippings. As there weren't any loose chippings all the drivers ignored the sign and continued going at about 40 mph.

Then another sign told us we could step up to 30 mph, but a little further on the limit went down to 10 again. By this time the motorists must have wondered what was coming next.

What came next was about 2 miles further on - and it was loose chippings at last, so the motorists slowed down to 20 of their own accord. They didn't want to spoil the paintwork on their cars!

There are several issues here. Why are signs which no longer apply left up on Britain's roads? Then there is the serious question as to whether the drivers who ignored the signs were right not to slow down. If they weren't, could or should they have been prosecuted? Do the people who leave misleading signs up expect drivers to use their common sense and act accordingly? Or should *they* be censured for misleading the public, and creating (or encouraging) a less than respectful approach to important notices?

But the business of giving misleading messages isn't just confined to the roads. Misleading messages come from politicians, statesmen, journalists and even preachers.

Some preachers tell their congregations that if they donate a lot of money to the cause, God will ensure that they become rich (financially) in return. That's not true. Others suggest that if you live a good life you will avoid hardship. Nonsense!

Perhaps cruellest of all is the person who suggests that if you have enough faith you will be cured of your illness whatever it is. But that's a distortion of the truth, and ignores the fact that the Great Healer sometimes decides our best healing is to take us to himself.

Like the misleading road sign other misleading messages can influence us to ignore the reliable ones. But reliable ones do exist. The gospels - which speak of God's love for us - are full of reliable messages. Let me encourage you to read them because they are well worth using as signposts for life.

Today's text: John 21:31 'These are written that you may believe that Jesus is the Christ, the Son of God, and that by believing you may have life in his name.' (NIV)

52

27
It's in the family

I'M glad we had our children while we were young. We've enjoyed them growing up while we've still been fit enough to play with them. These days our games of football, cricket, tennis and golf have a real keen edge.

The boys often say to me, 'Dad, the games are much better now. We're improving all the time - and you're getting worse.' Unfortunately they're right. But I'm still holding out - just.

It's fascinating to see them in action. And I have to admit that when I see them using tactics that I taught them I have a warm glow inside. Well, that is until they use them against me!

Last summer I was on the opposite cricket team to Mark, our eldest son. He had to bowl the last over against my side. We needed only a few runs to win, but I knew that Mark had been taught how to bowl so that batsmen would find it difficult to hit the ball. So what happened? Mark employed my tactics against *my* team, and beat us!

Family likenesses, traits and mannerisms can be fascinating. Probably our family's most significant characteristic is our Christian faith. The Christian values I was taught as a boy within my family have been of immense help. I will always be grateful.

But, of course, everyone can belong to God's family, and if we choose to accept God as our

Father there are certain characteristics which ought to draw us together and even show a 'family likeness'.

Jesus spelt out some of the attitudes and characteristics God expects from us. In the sermon on the mount he says, 'Love your enemies. bless those who curse you, do good to those who hate you, and pray for those who despitefully use you and persecute you...that *you may be the children of your Father* who is in heaven.'

He doesn't say *tolerate* your enemies. He says love them. He doesn't say *put up with* those who hate you, he says do good to them. He tells us to speak kindly to those who curse us and even to pray for people who work against us.

These family requirements are demanding.

It isn't *easy* to be a true child of God. But it's worth trying.

Today's text: Ephesians 3:14,15 'I kneel before the Father, from who his whole family in heaven and on earth derives its name.' (NIV)

28
Something about you-know-who

LAST Christmas we were introduced to a new table game. We tried it out round my brother John's house.

The idea of the game was that a word was held up behind a contestant while someone gave the contestant clues about the word. There was one golden rule. The person giving clues was not allowed to mention any part of the word being guessed at any time. To do so meant disqualification.

I sometimes think that half the population of England is playing a similar game. You see, there's a definite reluctance for people to speak about You-Know-Who. If you mention his name in ordinary conversation you're liable to be thought of as a crank or a religious maniac. It just isn't done - at least, not in polite company.

Even some preachers seem to be drawn into playing the game. When they're given air time on radio or television they seem to skirt around the main subject of their faith and leave 'his name' unspoken.

It's OK to speak about moral issues, social conditions, ethics and the state of the world, but to talk about You-Know-Who is not good form. I often marvel at the way preachers throw away their opportunities. And perhaps Christians do it in everyday life too.

It could be that some people have overdone it and used this person's name a little too often. They haven't managed to speak about him in a natural way, so others have written them off. Whatever the case, it's true that the mere mention of the word 'Jesus', oops, I've said it - sends some people running away as fast as they can go.

I'm not sure what all the fear is about. It might be that we want to keep Jesus at a distance because we know his goodness shows up our faults. It might be that Christianity asks us to be committed. There are probably as many different reasons as there are people running away.

What I know is this - that whenever he's welcomed into a life he changes it for the better. Jesus is worth talking about.

Today's text: Philippians 2:10,11   'At the name of Jesus every knee shall bow...and every tongue confess that Jesus Christ is Lord.' (NIV)

29
Who am I?

IF I were to ask you what temperament type you are, what would you say?

I mean, are you extrovert or introvert? Are you the kind of person who gets things moving or someone who naturally assumes it's nothing to do with you?

Recently, while on a course in London, I had my temperament type analysed. After I'd answered a long series of questions, my assessor decided my temperament could be summed up with four individual letters - E N F P. That's short for Extrovert, Intuitive, Feeling, Perceptive. And, cutting a long story short, it probably explains why I'm happy to talk to you this morning rather than drive quietly to an office desk and keep myself to myself.

I was also told that people like me don't often notice *things*. Quite right, I thought. If you were to ask me the colour or pattern of the wallpaper or carpets in my own home, I doubt I'd be able to tell you many at all.

But if I don't notice *things*, I do notice *people* - which is just as well, because people, not things, are my business. And the course I was on was designed to help me understand people better - especially those who think, react and judge differently from me.

I came away thinking it would do everybody good to go on the course. After all, there's more than enough misunderstanding, intolerance and confrontation around. And anything that helps us understand ourselves and others better can only be good.

Someone once said, 'To know all is to forgive all'. When we realise why others act the way they do, we have a greater likelihood of being generous and understanding towards them.

Three thousand years ago the psalmist prayed, 'Search me O God and know my thoughts. See if there is any offensive way in me, and lead me in the way everlasting.' (Psalm 139)

We can't all go on the course. But - like the psalmist - we can ask *God* to help us understand ourselves (and others) better and let him help us with the business of becoming what we ought to be.

Today's text: 1 Corinthians 13:12   'My knowledge now is partial; then it will be whole, like God's knowledge of me.' (NIV)

30
On a Sunday

I'M not a great expert on songs, but of all the days in the week it seems to me that Sunday gets written and sung about more than any other.

'Never, never on a Sunday' probably tops the list, but the song that gets home to me is, 'Tell me on a Sunday'. It's one of Andrew Lloyd Webber's. Sung by Elaine Paige, it tells the story of a woman who knows that her relationship with her partner is breaking up. She knows it's over and it's only a matter of his telling her.

But she doesn't want to be told in the wrong way. If breaking up is hard to do, this young lady still wants some dignity in it. So she pleads not to be told when her man has had too much to drink, or when he's in a temper - or just by a late night phone call.

She wants to be told tenderly, honestly. So she asks to be taken to a park lined with trees and be told - on a Sunday please.

Now, it's not always easy telling people what they don't want to hear. If you've ever had to break the news of the death of a loved one you'll know what I mean.

Then there are times when we simply don't want to hurt our friends by telling them the truth - you're not good enough to get the job, or to get into the team. Apparently there's one thing nobody ever tells their best friend...something to do with body odour, I think.

I suppose God must have tried thousands of ways of telling us things about ourselves. Especially things we wouldn't want to hear. If he's going to help us at all, we've got to be prepared to hear the truth - and that's probably why a lot of us keep him at a 'respectable' distance.

Even when Jesus was on earth, he found it difficult to get people to take in what they needed to hear. In the end he told us what he wanted us to know most of all, by giving his life for us. His death on a cross spoke louder than all the words he had used, and much clearer than any words I can use. But some of us can't be told anything, can we?

Even so, if we take time this weekend to see if God has anything to say to us he'll be there - ready to speak to us, in a Church service perhaps - telling us what he knows we each need to hear. Mind you, he can do that anywhere, any time - it doesn't *have* to be on a Sunday.

Today's text: John 3:16 *'God so loved the world that he gave his only son, that whoever believes in him shall not perish but have eternal life.'* (NIV)

31
God is no bully

A FEW weeks ago I was asked to fill in a questionnaire, and one of the questions was. 'What was the proudest moment of your life?' I knew what was the *happiest* - my wedding day. And the most *indescribable* moment was when I held our first child Nicola in my arms two minutes after she was born. But the *proudest*? It's back to my daughter again. My *proudest* moment, I decided, was when I walked her down the aisle in September 1991.

To see her on the day, radiant in her wedding dress, you wouldn't imagine she was the same girl who once sorted out the school bully. For months, one particular girl had punched and bossed her way around the girls' school and one day Nicola decided she wouldn't take any more.

She refused to be pushed around this time and, when she was attacked, she showed the bully who was boss. The teachers were delighted. They told me so. Even congratulated me(!) because discipline became better at school after that.

It's never easy knowing when to retaliate and deal with bullies. Sometimes we feel it makes us as bad as them. On the other hand, if we don't show some kind of defence, we run the risk of everything getting out of control - either at school, at home, at work, in government or even between countries.

What we can be sure about is that God has told us to leave any *vengeful* sorting out to him. Ultimately he will put things right. All injustices will be shown up.

If we find that difficult to accept, let's remind ourselves that our all-powerful God never bullies *us* in any way. If he wanted to bully us into obeying and loving him, he wouldn't have given his life on a cross. Far from getting annoyed with us and forcing us to do his will, he says, 'I love you so much that I am willing to be killed for you.'

Jesus gives each of us the freedom to choose to accept him as Lord and Saviour - or not. He used no bullying tactics when he was on earth, and he doesn't use any now.

Today's text: Revelation 3:20 'Here I stand knocking at the door; if anyone hears my voice and opens the door, I will come in and sit down to supper with him and he with me.' (NEB)

32
Wimbledon

I WANT to suggest, while Wimbledon is with us, that Jesus would have made a brilliant tennis player.

He always knew how to put the ball back into the other person's court - and win.

Take the time when an expert in the law tried to wrong foot him in public.

The expert began with an ace. 'What must I do to inherit eternal life?' he asked. *15-0.*

But instead of starting on some long discourse, Jesus put the ball back in the teacher's court. 'You tell me,' he said. 'What's written in the law?' *15 all.*

The teacher knew his stuff. Back came the reply: 'Love the lord your God with all your heart and with all your soul and with all your strength and with all your mind, and love your neighbour as yourself.'

Superb! It was the perfect answer. *30-15* to the teacher.

But instead of being humiliated, Jesus was still dictating the play. 'You've answered correctly,' he said. 'Do this and you will live.' He had told the teacher what to do! *30 all.*

The teacher wasn't enjoying this. trick Jesus, so he made another attempt at putting the ball back in Jesus' court. Having been told to love his neighbour as himself, he asked, 'And who is my neighbour?'

40-30 to the teacher.

There then follows what I can only call a long rally as Jesus relates the parable of the Good Samaritan and how this man - from a race the teacher despised - went to the aid of a traveller who had been mugged, while other religious men passed by on the other side.

At the end of the story Jesus put the ball back in the teacher's court by asking him who was neighbour to the mugged traveller. *Deuce*.

This was the master-stroke, because whatever the teacher might have thought about the story, he didn't want to use the word 'Samaritan' in any praiseworthy way. So he gave a feeble reply and merely referred to the Samaritan as 'the one who had mercy on him.' He'd let himself down badly. The *advantage* was now with Jesus, who wrapped it all up by commanding 'Go and do likewise!' *Game, Set and Match*, you might say.

The teacher knew all the theory about living. But when it came to putting his beliefs into practice - that was another story.

If Jesus were telling the parable to us today I think he'd make a Muslim or a Catholic or a Protestant - or some particular person or group we just can't get on with - the star of the show, rather than a Samaritan. And when we'd got the message he'd tell *us* to 'Go, and do likewise!'

Today's text: 1 John 3:18 'Let us not love with words or tongue but with actions and in truth.' (NIV)

64

33
Not going anywhere

ONE of Ronnie Barker's best TV sketches has him standing in front of a map of Britain introducing a new motorway system. All the roads bypass all the towns. It was designed that way, said Ronnie, so you could drive all day without going anywhere.

Last weekend I was sitting in someone's house when I saw a tramp on a TV film trying to thumb a lift. The card he held up said 'Anywhere'. He didn't have any preferences for his destination, he just knew he didn't want to be where he was.

I reckon there are more than a few people like him. They'd give anything to be in another situation. They have had enough. It's too tough. They aren't appreciated where they are so what's the point?

We all know what it's like to be in the wrong place at the wrong time for all the wrong reasons, when we just wish the ground would open up and swallow us. If only we could be somewhere else! Anywhere. Like the hapless 'star' footballers who miss their penalties in the shoot outs. They'd give anything to be somewhere else. Anywhere - except on that football pitch in front of the empty goal.

But there are other people who'd go anywhere for different reasons. We've heard today of illegal immigrants moving from country to country trying to find somewhere to live. We've also heard of a mother whose baby has been kidnapped. She would literally travel anywhere if it means getting her baby back. People with a loved one who's critically ill would also go anywhere if it meant a cure could be found.

That kind of adventurous spirit is quite different from the tramp's idea of just going 'anywhere'. His idea is aimless, pointless, lacking direction. So is Ronnie Barker's drive. That goes nowhere.

On Saturday I was at the burial of a very brave woman who had spent her last few years suffering from cancer. Her difficulties didn't defeat her. She knew where she was going. She had an *ultimate* destination. She believed she was going to meet a God who had strengthened and guided her at every turn.

Jesus Christ promised that God would guide ordinary people like you and me - that he would stay with us right to the end and beyond.

I know some people find that easier to believe than others, but with help like that, none of us need be going just 'anywhere'.

Today's text*: Psalm 23:6. 'Surely goodness and mercy shill follow me all the days of my life: and I will dwell in the house of the Lord for ever.'* (AV)

34
How much are you worth?

YESTERDAY I met the daughter of one of my predecessors. Edward Joy was The Salvation Army Divisional Commander for Norfolk nearly 80 years ago. His daughter Marjory remembers him buying one of her treasured possessions from Norwich market in 1917. It was a bust of John Wesley. Her father paid two shillings for it - quite a price for the time. She imagines it would be worth quite a lot these days, but she's never found out.

Even so, I doubt if it's worth five million pounds. That's what the asking price is today for Chris Sutton. He is available from another Norwich market - the football transfer market. I'd be surprised if Chris Sutton thought he was worth that much, even in football terms. And if he does get paid £12,000 a week, as some agencies have reported, nobody's worth can be measured by the size of his wages.

The spending of five million on a footballer raises a few questions about values - including how else the money could have been spent. If you had five million pounds how would you spend it? Perhaps some could go on a brand new, classy car, or on a larger house, or a round the world cruise - and still have some left for a rainy day.

We all have personal choices to make about the way we finance our lives and we can sometimes be distastefully indulgent compared with much of the rest of the world. If we could be transported to some less wealthy societies I feel sure we'd rearrange some of our values and adopt a simpler life style.

Cynics suggest that when it comes to values every man has his price. They say there is a point at which everyone would sell him or herself. Standards and morals would be forsaken for the price of something we desperately want but do not yet possess.

We could argue all day as to whether or not they're right, but it's worth remembering that God himself put a price on our lives. He decided how much we were worth - how much, in fact, he'd pay for us, backing up all he said about caring for us. Jesus Christ gave his life for us. He paid the supreme price for our wrongdoing.

If at times we're prone to underestimate our own worth, we're invited to remember that God values us as being worth all he has.

Today's text: Matthew 10:31 *'So do not be afraid; you are worth much more than many sparrows!'* (GNB)

35

Christmas rush - in Bethlehem

SOME people reckon they wouldn't want to go to Bethlehem in case their Christmas card image of the place where Jesus was born was shattered.

I went for the first time 10 years ago and although I've been back a couple of times since, including this year, I have to admit that my first impression of Bethlehem was one of disappointment.

It's such a poor place. Many shops are either boarded up or closed down. Then there's the graffiti. You might see a few soldiers too, and sense political unrest. And it's true that you don't see green fields with angels and bright lights. But you do get a picture of the world into which Jesus was born - the real world.

It eventually dawns on you that Bethlehem was a deprived area where there was political unrest, with Roman soldiers and King Herod both making life very difficult.

Just as significant for me was the behaviour of some of the pilgrims. Just as there was no room for Mary, Joseph and Jesus at the inn, so there were more people wanting to enter the little room where tradition says Jesus was born than the room could accommodate. Some of the pilgrims were pushing in and shoving us around hoping they'd get into the room more quickly and it wasn't very dignified.

But while all this was going on a young couple were kneeling together, quietly praying to the God who had come to earth as a baby. They somehow managed to remain oblivious to all the noise and bustle round them, and they worshipped. I don't know who they were or which country they came from, but they provided a timely reminder of what the coming of Jesus was all about.

Most of us know what it's like to get pushed or shoved around in a shopping centre at Christmas and it's pretty obvious that the Christmas rush can crowd out time for concentrating on what the birth of Jesus means.

Christmas is about God coming to save us from ourselves. It's about God identifying himself with us. It's about God showing and giving us love - unconditionally.

Don't let Christmas go by without some moment of worship or adoration. If you do you'll have missed the real point.

Today's text: Psalm 95:6 'Come, let us bow down in worship, let us kneel before the Lord our Maker; for he is our God.' (NIV)

36
A right pantomime

TODAY marks the end of the Christmas holidays. It's back to normal - whatever that is. Children have gone to school, adults are back at work and it's time to do something about our waistlines.

Even so, the pantomime season is still with us with its upside- down world in which the leading male role is played by a woman and the dame is played by a friendly old man or someone like that.

I'm told that the concept of pantomime was introduced centuries ago when the Feast of Fools took over village life for a holiday period. It was a kind of medieval 'Trading places'. The lord of the manor became a servant, and 'lesser lights' took over the running of things. I've no idea how successful the feast was, but I can imagine this upside-down world could have created a few problems for when people resumed their normal roles.

News reviews of the year give us chance to take a look at how things are being run by those in charge and I've no doubt that some of us reckon we could do better - given the chance, of course.

Sometimes we look at the world and think it's already upside-down. The innocent suffer; bullies escape; terrorists seem to have the upper hand; victims are left unhelped while offenders are treated to holidays; there's one rule for the rich and another for the poor. But this isn't new. Three thousand

71

years ago a psalmist complained bitterly to God that the wicked and powerful always seemed to get away with things.

When Jesus came he turned things upside-down again. He said things like, 'Love your enemies. Do good to those who hate you. Bless those who curse you. Pray for people who are just plain nasty to you and give you a rough time.'

He knew full well that these positive responses aren't necessarily our natural first reaction. But if we were to let our baser instincts dictate all the time we'd have a right pantomime on our hands, and in certain parts of the world that sadly is what has happened.

The teaching of Jesus may not be easy to put into practice, but it is the only way to make our world a better place.

Oh no, it isn't? Oh yes, it is!

Today's text: *Matthew 7:24 'Everyone who hears these words of mine and puts them into practice is like a wise man who built his house on the rock.' (NIV)*

37
Want to argue about it?

BEING a football manager is a precarious
occupation. If your team is winning, the players are
usually given the credit. If your team is losing, you
quickly become a target for personal abuse, until
you are eventually sacked and replaced.

Mike Walker did a good job for Norwich City, so
I could understand why fans and directors alike
didn't want him to accept an offer from another
club.

Unfortunately, passions ran high and more than a
few harsh words were spoken, arguments took place,
and much of the good work was forgotten for a
time.

Football has more than its fair share of arguments
and cool heads are often missing in the heat of the
moment.

Take the abandoned match at Manchester City
with City leading Ipswich 2-0. The referee's decision
to pronounce the pitch unplayable and call off the
match was just too much for City goalkeeper Tony
Coton. He raced up to the ref, shouted at him,
waved his arms at him, then pushed him, then
nearly exploded. The ref exercised remarkable
restraint and Coton later apologised - profusely.

But the crowd argued too. They even turned on
their own manager, who pleaded with them to
accept the fact that the pitch was so wet it was like

a lake.

Last week a referee abandoned a boys' match - not because the *lads* were doing anything wrong, but because their *parents* were arguing on the touch line. The language had reached such a pitch that the ref decided the boys would be better served if he called proceedings to a halt.

So does all this arguing reflect a current lack of acceptance of authority and decisions by the rest of us? Do we push hard for whatever we can get and react badly if things go against us? Or dare we suggest it's just a football problem?

I think, if we're honest, most of us would have to confess to sometimes arguing against what's best for us - arguing against good rulings. Sometimes it's with our parents, perhaps our boss, and even God - and we'd do well to check ourselves over especially on the last one.

On the other hand, you might disagree. Want to argue about it?

Today's text: Romans 8:31 'What, then, shall we say in response to this? If God is for us, who can be against us?' (NIV)

74

38
Not so easy

IT'S easy to point out that a government minister shouldn't father a child through an extra-marital relationship. It's easy to condemn a joy-rider who allegedly runs over a helpless policewoman - twice. It's easy to feel anger as well. It's easy to blame teenagers for the rise in juvenile crime and condemn parents for their lack of guidance, for not being available and having little sense of discipline. It's easy to point out that a mother of 59 who gives birth to twins through donated eggs, and at vast expense, is not going to be around for long enough to be a good mother to her children. And it's especially easy to tell other people how they should bring up their children.

All these situations have occurred in the Year of the Family and, not surprisingly, opinions as to the value of family life are flowing thick and fast. If a BBC poll is to be believed, 41 per cent of girls are sexually experienced before they reach the age of 16, the age of consent, and more than a third of all children born in Britain are born to women who are not married. So it's easy to see that the values and traditional structure which added stability to life a generation or two ago are in real danger of being lost - at least, for the foreseeable future.

But it's *not* so easy to be an exemplary parent, or a perfect child, or a forgiving partner. It's not easy to stand up for Christian values and make sure your life matches your words. It's not easy always doing what is right.

I didn't grow up in an anti-establishment culture. Today's teenagers do. Films are usually one step ahead of the law, one step smarter, and often with the end justifying some pretty questionable means. I didn't grow up with pop videos showing seductive sex symbols all the time. Today's families have to accept that media and peer pressure put extra demands on parents and children alike. The trouble is that everybody needs looking after and caring for, but nobody has the time to do it. The guidance and time children need just isn't there - at least, not often enough.

If we're going to take family values seriously, we each need to look first, not somewhere else, but at our own contributions to the stability of life around us.

That isn't as easy as telling other people how to run their lives - but it's a great deal more important.

Today's text: *Titus 2:11* *'For the grace of God has dawned upon the world with healing for all mankind; and by it we are disciplined to renounce godless ways and worldly desires, and to live a life of temperance, honesty, and godliness in the present age.'* *(NEB)*

39
My idea of Heaven

I SUPPOSE we all have a different idea of what we'd like Heaven to be. My idea of Heaven is playing cricket on a village green on a summer's afternoon. For me cricket has everything - pace, bravery, skill, competition, individual performance, planning, team work and something close to peace and serenity.

If Heaven really was a place where cricket was played, I imagine Brian Johnston would be very much at home there. Give him a microphone and it would be - well, Paradise. Strangely enough, Brian has just been advertising holidays in Paradise - the West Indian one where England will shortly be playing their next test series. But Brian won't be there. As we all know, he died earlier this week after never fully recovering from a heart attack.

I met Brian just once. It was a brief meeting at Lord's and it was only of the autograph variety when he kindly responded to my lads' request. But the encounter was enough to show that what people have said about him always being the same friendly person in real life as he was on the TV was true. And there have been some very special tributes this week.

Former England captain Ray Illingworth said that Brian, a public schoolboy and Oxford graduate, always had the knack of making everyone feel valued. He treated everyone with equal respect. It was something that Illingworth - a Yorkshire lad with a Yorkshire accent - said made a big impression on him. Illingworth's words set me thinking that Heaven is a place where everyone has equal respect and we all discover how much we are valued. It would make sense because, however talented we are, however rich or famous, however slow or poor, God tells us we are valued equally.

I think Heaven will be a great leveller. The proud, the people who think they've earned a place, those who reckon they've done the world a favour, will find they're on a sticky wicket. According to Jesus they'll discover that their own goodness wasn't nearly so good as they thought. Others who perhaps never got a look in, or never imagined the part they played counted for much, will discover that when Jesus said the first would be last and the last first, he meant it.

Nobody will manage to prove there is a Heaven - not while we're living here anyway - but a place where God eventually puts everything into perspective, and rights wrongs, seems to round things off logically to me. It makes sense and gives depth to the variety of experiences we all encounter while we have our innings here.

Today's text: Mark 9:35 'If anyone wants to be first, he must be the very last, and the servant of all.' (NIV)

40
Back to square one

WHAT I wanted for my birthday was a pair of football boots.

Some of my friends at our local Salvation Army had arranged to play a football match that day and they'd invited me to take part. It didn't matter to them that I was 43. They thought I could get through the 90 minutes. So I told my mother I wanted a pair of football boots.

She said everything I expected her to say. That I was too old. That I ought to grow up. That I ought to accept the inevitable. And, yes, she would buy me the football boots.

I decided to play in my old position which we used to call left-wing. It meant that I could have a rest every now and then and no one would realise if I was getting tired. Cutting a long story short, we won 5-0 and I scored a goal. (Actually, it would have been difficult *not* to score on this occasion.)

But my mother was right. Time is rapidly moving on. I have to watch more sport these days and participate a little less.

Sports coverage in the media has come a long way from those first live commentaries on the Light Programme (as it was called). I wasn't around for those, but someone who was tells me that when football match commentaries first began, a plan of the pitch was printed in the *Radio Times*. The plan had numbered squares on it. While the commentator carried out his duties, somebody else would chip in with 'Square one' or 'Square seven'. It was fascinating stuff and helped the listeners build up an authentic picture of what was happening.

So, if a player was in trouble and needed to pass the ball back to his goalkeeper, the commentator's helper would announce 'Square one'. My friend is convinced that's where the saying came from - 'Back to square one'.

Sometimes I think I'd like to go back to square one with my footballing - to be young again, so that I could play more often. In other areas of life too I have sometimes wanted to go back to square one and start all over again.

What saddens me is meeting people who have made a mess of things, and can't or won't forgive themselves. They say they've let the side down badly - usually it's their family or friends. Things can't be put right.

Well, that may be true, but there isn't any point in staying defeated. The Christian gospel has at its heart the message of a second chance. And a third and fourth chance - more, if necessary.

When we can't forgive ourselves it is vital to remember that God does. He can't take us back to square one, but he can and does give us a fresh start.

Today's text: 1 John 1:9 'If we confess our sins to God...he will forgive us our sins and purify us from our wrongdoing.' (GNB)

41

If you don't love me I'll kill you

I'LL never forget the day I became a dad. I remember it as if it were yesterday. Within minutes of my daughter's birth she was carefully wrapped in a blanket and placed in my arms. As I looked at the warm, lovable, dependent bundle I was holding I knew my world had changed for ever.

What I didn't realise was how much our children would help keep me in touch with the rest of the world. As my wife and I have tried to teach the three of them and help them develop their own characters, we have also learned a great deal from them.

For instance, in my time as editor of *The War Cry* they helped me keep up to date with what was going on. If they thought one of the latest pop songs had the right kind of slant for Christian comment they'd make sure I knew.

But through the years they have *inadvertently* helped me as well.

When that warm, lovable, dependent bundle was five years old she had a brother who was three. One evening just after I'd arrived home I watched her put her arms around him and tell him that she loved him. His reply was an uncomplimentary 'Get off'. But she wasn't deterred. She told him again that she loved him. Again he merely said 'Get off'. She told him again. The response was the same.

Finally, in desperation, she shouted at him, 'If you don't love me, I'll kill you!' I then watched as her three-year-old brother decided to play dead. He was hoping she'd go away. But she didn't. She jumped on him. A fight started and I had to intervene. What had started as a loving action had turned into something completely different.

But it was those words 'If you don't love me I'll kill you' that stayed with me. I knew I'd heard them somewhere before. And then I realised it was from preachers who had a very negative idea of the love of God. Somehow they had managed to give their listeners the impression that God was such an angry God that if we didn't do everything he said, he would get rid of us - kill us, send us to Hell. Well, that's one way of expressing what is called the 'good news'.

But it seems to me there's a more positive way of re-telling the story of God's love. And it's this. At the heart of the Christian gospel is the fact that Jesus Christ - God's son - came to earth and *gave his life* for us. He said, in effect, 'I love you so much that I will be killed for you'.

It was Jesus himself who told us about God's love and it was Jesus who proved it.

Today's text: *John 3:16   'God loved the world so much that he gave his only Son, so that everyone who believes in him may not die but have eternal life.'* (GNB)

42

Reason to believe

SOME people find it easy to believe in God. They have no difficulty. It's as natural to them as breathing. Other people say they couldn't believe in God if you gave them a million pounds.

The Salvation Army's newspaper *The War Cry* has both kinds of readers. When I was editor we invited them to tell us what made it easy or what made it difficult for them to believe in God.

Three main reasons for *not* believing emerged. One was the bad example of Christians. Some of our readers recalled instances where they had been let down by people who called themselves Christians.

The second reason for not believing in God was that he hadn't answered prayer. God - if he existed - had apparently chosen to ignore them or he hadn't answered in the way they wanted.

The third reason for not believing in God was suffering. It's the one I would have put at the top of my list. Watching a loved one suffer, said one of my friends to me recently, is the most horrific human experience I can think of.

When we looked at reasons as to why people found belief in God relatively *easy* the answers went like this.

First - the good example of Christians. Our readers said they had been so impressed by

Christian friends that they had wanted to become Christians themselves.

Another reason for believing was answer to prayer. When they had asked God for help, it had come. They were convinced of his activity in their lives. He was not deaf, nor was he uncaring.

The third reason people had for believing was suffering, yes, suffering. When either they or a loved one had been in great pain or had had to endure something that was unfair or traumatic, they had sensed the presence of God in a special and powerful way. The God who had himself suffered on the cross, and felt pain, loneliness and rejection, was there to help them in their moment of need.

And so our survey involved exactly the same three areas for *not* believing in God as it did for believing in God.

One of my friends says he would love to believe in God but he can't. He says he's been conditioned not to believe since an early age. He's been taught to be suspicious of anything religious.

I know it's hard, terribly hard, for some people to believe. But Jesus promised that those who seek will find. We should never give up.

Today's text: Mark 9:23,24. *'Jesus said, 'Everything is possible for him who believes.'*
Immediately the boy's father exclaimed, 'I do believe; help me overcome my unbelief!' ' (NIV)

43
In safe hands

EVERYONE knows what it feels like to be a new boy (or girl). When I made my first trip into New York I knew I was a new boy, but I had a friend who was assigned to help me. He was a fellow Salvation Army officer and it was his job to take me round to some of the Salvation Army's Social Services centres in that city.

He was kind, but I didn't feel entirely safe in his hands. He wasn't what I would call 'streetwise'. He came from America's deep south and hadn't been in the New York area long. He had that innocent look about him that the city types can spot a mile off.

Well, I was in his hands, and when he took me to a particularly rough area of New York to see the 400 or so men who were being cared for at Booth House, I could tell he was struggling. He never said so and he was the perfect host.

Booth House was nowhere near so magnificent as the other Salvation Army centres I had seen. But it was a place where all those who didn't fit in anywhere else were welcome. Perhaps the most honest way of summing up the men who were there would be to call them 'inadequate'. Some had a drugs problem, some an alcohol problem, some both. Some had mental and emotional problems, some had had breakdowns and some just couldn't cope.

But it was the centre which impressed me most of all. One of the reasons for this was Tom. He was a radiant, 'full of life' kind of person, and was in charge of helping rehabilitate the men.

During my afternoon at Booth House, residents kept putting their arms around him and telling me how great he was. Tom had made them feel worth something.

While I was with him he pulled out an old photograph of himself. 'Look,' he said. 'That was me six years ago. Now look at me!' I could see what he was trying to tell me. The man in the photograph - the man who used to be a drug user and pusher, the man who was once an alcoholic and down-and-out - that was the man in the photograph. The face bore practically no resemblance to the Tom who stood in front of me now - a changed man, a whole-hearted Christian.

The men in that centre felt safe in Tom's hands. I felt safe in Tom's hands in that rough area of New York. As for Tom, he had put himself into the hands of God six years previously and what a difference it had made!

If we place ourselves in God's hands - wherever we are and even if we die - we're sure to be in the safest place of all.

Today's text: Proverbs 3:5 'Put all your trust in the Lord, and do not rely on your own understanding.' (REB)

44

I gave her away

I HAVE just given my daughter away. After all the time, money and care given to her for 21 years, I gave her away!

I didn't get a penny for her. She must be worth a few bob - but no, I just had to pay the bills again.

And that's how it should be. I may have been responsible for her welfare all these years, but that doesn't make her my property.

She's a person. And her worth cannot be measured in cash terms.

And yet I did get some reward from the day - a great deal of reward. If she doesn't mind me saying so, her happy smiling face made everything worthwhile.

I knew she was contented - and grateful. That was enough.

A special feature of that day was that the person who conducted the marriage ceremony also conducted our daughter's dedication ceremony when she was given back to God as a baby. You see, we'd 'given her away' before. Or rather, we'd given her back to God. We'd acknowledged that she belonged to him and was a gift from him. And all this set me thinking about the day God gave his Son away - to the world.

For him it wasn't the happy 'hand over' occasion of the kind we enjoyed when Nicola became

Matthew's wife. When God gave his Son to the world, he knew we would kill him - that Jesus would die a cruel death, that he would be rejected, lonely and despairing. This 'giving away' was costly.

Why did God do it - especially when it was so painful? The Bible's answer goes like this:

'God loved the world so much that he gave his only Son, that everyone who has faith in him may not die but have eternal life.' (*John 3:16*)

Seeing us happy, contented and grateful for his love would certainly make his giving worth it, don't you think? So would receiving our love in return.

Today's text: 1 John 4:10 'This is love; not that we loved God, but that he loved us and sent his Son as an atoning sacrifice for our sins.' (NIV)

45
Injustice

ONE of the favourite pastimes of football fans is complaining about the referee. We even have radio phone-in programmes to do it now.

When we feel let down or cheated, we seem to need someone to blame. It can be a sign of immaturity, but there are also times when injustice needs to be confronted and defeated.

I remember one football match when every decision the referee made seemed designed to stop our team playing and help the other team win. In the end our team lost patience, then lost heart and then lost the game. I remember feeling a great sense of injustice that night and so did a young lad who was with me.

An ambulance flashed past us soon after the match had finished and the lad said, 'I hope the referee is in there.' His sense of injustice was obviously keen as well, and I had to tell him that however badly he felt the referee had refereed, he needed to learn how to control his feelings.

But if men and boys, and women and girls, can get het up over a football match, how do we think people who suffer deep injustices in war-torn, famine-stricken countries feel? Or don't we think much about their emotions? Their sense of injustice is real. The right kind of remedy is needed. Frequently they need 'outside' help.

But what about our own complaints about injustice? Sometimes they are aimed at the police, or the council, our employer, or even people at home. There are occasions we want to blame the referee as it were - whoever it happens to be. And sometimes we too feel powerless to do anything.

It might not solve my problems, but it helps me to remember that nobody suffered more injustice than the Son of God. Accused of crimes he hadn't done, mocked even for healing people and condemned to a cruel death for living a good life, Jesus Christ certainly knows all about the kind of things we might complain about. He also knows how to listen to our claims and concerns.

If today you are feeling really bad about some injustice, he's well worth talking to.

Today's text: Isaiah 53:4,5 'Surely he took up our infirmities and carried our sorrows....He was pierced for our transgressions, he was crushed for our iniquities; the punishment that brought us peace was upon him.' (NIV)

46
Climbing Snowdon

I'VE climbed Snowdon four times. The first time was when our children Nicola and Mark were five and three respectively. I had Mark on my shoulders most of the way, but we made it to the top.

Twelve years later we made another trip. This time Tony (our third child) was with us. He was 10. At first he wasn't too keen. He made very excuse he could think of not to go on the climb, but in the end he reluctantly started the ascent.

Just after halfway, when the track began to get steep, I realised he was getting ahead of us. He'd suddenly become quite keen to get to the summit first.

I decided to leave the others and catch him up I could see that thick clouds were gathering near the top and I didn't want Tony to get lost in them.

But try as I might I couldn't catch him up. And it suddenly became a significant day in my life. I'd just turned 40 and I had to accept that my 10-year-old son was not going to be caught by his not-so-fit father.

In time Tony disappeared into the clouds. I kept climbing as fast as I could.

When I reached the clouds I hadn't gone many paces into them before I saw Tony, sitting on a rock, waiting patiently for me.

'Where have you been?' he said. 'I've been

waiting for ages.'

I'm not sure how I replied to him, but what happened next was that he put his hand in mine and together we trod the track that I had been along before.

Eventually we came out of the clouds and were greeted by bright sunshine. Then he raced off and beat me to the summit.

There are other times when the clouds seem to come over us and make the way ahead seem either gloomy or at best uncertain. In such times it's not a bad idea to take time to know that God our Father, is with us.

If we put our hand in his we can be sure he knows the way through and, eventually (even ultimately) he will lead us into the sunshine of his love.

It might take patience and a measure of trust, but there's no better guide and no surer way of reaching our ultimate destination.

Today's text: Matthew 28:20 'Surely I am with you always, to the very end of the age.' (NIV)

47

Pollution

IF you're sitting in your car in a traffic jam on a cold January morning it isn't always wise to have the heater on. More than likely smoke is churning out of the exhaust of the car in front. If your heater is on the smoke is sucked into your car. It's just another sign of a modern problem - pollution.

The break-up of an oil tanker with 85,000 tons of oil pouring out on to the Shetlands coastline has been this week's pollution story.

It initially raised fears that puffins - the Shetland Islands' national emblem - could be wiped out, all 50,000 of them. Otters and seals have already died, as have hundreds of birds, including great northern divers, guillemots and shags. But, thankfully, the damage isn't as bad as was first thought and yesterday air quality round the wreck was better than in London.

This has been a major disaster, but we know that pollution is quietly doing its deadly work all over the place all the time. In recent years 24 billion tons of carbon dioxide have been added to our atmosphere annually. Eighty per cent of it has come from burning coal and gas, the rest from felling and burning tropical rain forests and this has its side line effect of killing thousands of species of plant, insect and animal life. Some progress is being made but we're aware that not enough of us take the matter seriously enough. All too often we expect other people to make the effort and the sacrifices.

If we dare to take this subject to its logical conclusion, we eventually have to admit that much of what makes our world mucky, dangerous and life-threatening is caused by the main pollution, the one that's everywhere, the one that claims us all.

Some people would call it sin, others may call it wrongdoing. In the end, this pollution boils down to selfishness. It is because we insist on treating and using the world in the way that suits us, rather than considering the wider effects, that pollution spreads.

Selfishness can - and does - pollute all of us in one way or another and it needs to be treated. It's just a case of being made clean on the inside.

So, it's back to the Creator - again.

Today's text: Psalm 51:10 'Create in me a clean heart, O God; and renew a right spirit within me.' (AV)

48
It's the losing that counts

THIS morning I'm breathing a sigh of relief. My football team won last night and escaped relegation. Luton Town were doing exceptionally well for a while. They even got to Wembley for the cup semi-final, but then fell at this last important hurdle, and after that their confidence went and they just kept losing.

What made matters worse for me was that so many other Salvation Army officers in the Eastern Counties seem to support Chelsea - the team which knocked us out of the cup. You learn things about your friends at times like these. Some people left cheeky messages on our answering machine, while the divisional youth secretary, who actually works in our offices, could hardly contain himself. His smile said it all. His team had won - my team had lost.

All this friendly teasing - well, I think it's friendly - is a bit like Ian Hislop's remark to fellow TV panellist Paul Merton, after his team, Ian's, had beaten Paul's last week. Ian said, 'It's not the winning that counts, it's the look on your face when you lose!'

So, on the 40th anniversary of Roger Bannister's record-breaking four-minute-mile, we need to remember that losing is an integral part of life. We can't avoid it. Even Bannister lost.

In recent years some well-meaning educationalists

have tried to protect children from losing games at school by not having games and winners. It seemed a futile exercise to me because life won't be so kind. We can't avoid disappointments and children need to be prepared for them.

Losing is good for us. We may not always like it or accept it, but we need to lose. Constant success isn't good for anybody. And from what I can see, Heaven is a place for losers.

According to Jesus Christ, it's for those who know they don't deserve to be there. It's for those who are prepared to admit they've been less than perfect, that they've made mistakes. In addition, they have asked for forgiveness and trust in God's goodness.

People who assume they're good enough have missed the point. 'Self-made' people have missed the point too. They've only made it with the talents God gave them anyway!

So this morning, let's thank God that he knows our limitations - and that when we fail he is always ready to help.

Today's text: Luke 15:21,22 'And the son said, 'Father, I have sinned against heaven and before you; I am no longer worthy to be called your son.'

But the Father said to his servants, 'Bring quickly the best robe and put it on him....' ' (RSV)

49
Political correctness

WAS Prince Charles right, or not? Yesterday he attacked the 'intellectual fanaticism' of political correctness, which he said was sweeping the country. Fashionable theories are undermining the fabric of society according to the Prince, and he pleaded for the general public to reject the self-appointed experts who had got it wrong.

How does political correctness manifest itself? Well, it's often found in the way we refer to, or treat, certain people or subjects in order to avoid giving offence. At what might be regarded as ultra-sensitive levels, some people would avoid talking about black coffee and refer to coffee without milk. My son says that instead of calling someone 'short', we now suggest that he (or she) might be 'vertically challenged'. It's true!

But when the story of the birth of Jesus is omitted by local authorities at Christmas to avoid offending people of other religions, something's gone wrong somewhere. We've actually thrown *the* baby out with the bath water. And it might be that fundamental trendy changes like that are the ones that the Prince objects to.

But there are slips in our everyday chatter that we sometimes need to check. Only yesterday, my secretary, Barbara, pointed out that I had inadvertently asked for some colleagues to

97

recommend 'a man' to be the director of a particular campaign I was arranging. 'Does it have to be a man?' she asked, with an innocent look on her face. She had made her point.

The political correctness debate will continue. But today as we are invited to vote in local elections, we might like to consider a different kind of political correctness.

Wouldn't it be wonderful if politicians got their forecasts correct? It would be even more wonderful if their promises proved to be correct!

Experience teaches us to be wary, to expect the worst, to distrust what we're being told and to say 'I told you so' when policies are changed to suit party political needs close to an election.

Now, although this isn't exactly the kind of political correctness which the Prince was talking about, I'd like to suggest that however good or bad we are at saying the right thing, we at least try to speak with truth and integrity. The politically correct lobby will remind us to speak with sensitivity too.

Today's text: Psalm 19:14 'May the words of my mouth and the meditation of my heart be pleasing in your sight, O Lord, my Rock and my Redeemer.' (NIV)

50
Don't give up!

WE'VE done it now. We've made a permanent land link with the Continent. We may have hidden it under the sea, but it's there. Today the Queen and President Mitterand are officially opening the Channel Tunnel. It cost 10 billion pounds and involved 15,000 workers.

For centuries invaders have been thwarted in their efforts to conquer our shores. From the autumn we'll invite them in with friendship.

Digging on the tunnel began in 1987 and within a few months the England end hit some problems. The rock began to break up and water started to seep through. The problems seemed almost insurmountable and a few hearts became faint, but machinery was modified and the digging went on until that highly-publicised day when British and French flags were exchanged somewhere under the Channel. The link was finally made.

These days we're probably a bit blasé about great engineering feats, but the opening of this tunnel - well, three tunnels, actually - is a credit to the skill, technology and vision of many people. Determination to succeed played an important part.

Last weekend two people fairly well-known to me were to be found on a beach near Lowestoft, trying to make the proverbial tunnel in the sand. The problem with these tunnels is that they have no firm structure and they keep on collapsing. Determination won that day. They just wouldn't give up.

But giving up is actually quite common these days. Marriage partners give up on each other at a higher rate than has ever been known, some parents give up on their children when behaviour patterns start to go wrong, some students give up study when the going gets tough, some people even give up on themselves.

But there are other examples shining through like modern-day Robert the Bruces. Think of the mediators in the Bosnian war. They work tirelessly for almost no return. Think of Roy Castle battling against cancer with the cheeriest of smiles imaginable. Think of his wife, Fiona, bravely supporting him.

Many of us have a tendency to give up when things are at their worst. But if we think about it, that's precisely the wrong time. A wise man once gave this advice for dark days: 'Never get out of the train in the tunnel.' We shouldn't give up just because we're having a bad time. There *is* light at the end of our tunnel.

Today's text: Matthew 24:13 'He who stands firm to the end will be saved.' (NIV)